05/30/2011

JAMAICA
0 20
0 12
Lucea
Montego Bay
Clark's Town
Ocho Rios
Port Maria
Negril
Savanna-la Mar
Cockpit Country
Dry Harbour Mountains
Buff Bay
Port Antonio
Blue Mtns
Black River
Alligator Pond
May Pen
Spanish Town
Kingston
Treasure Beach
Long Bay
Portland Bight
Caribbean Sea

Printed in the United States of America

ISBN:978-1-300-01292-4

LULU Press

3101 Hillsborough St.

Raleigh, NC 27607

Personal Message

To commemorate ***Jamaica's 50th year of independence*** *and her continued growth and prosperity, this book of specially written poetry is intended as my contribution to the upliftment of her name. These heart-felt poems are dedicated to Jamaicans at home and those away from home, as well as all our visitors and friends. Regardless of the challenges of a growing nation, we have much to be proud of, yet much to achieve. Great and many are the obstacles, but with a steadfast resolve from each patriotic Jamaican, and gratuity for the hard work of our leaders and nation builders- living and deceased, we will continue to make strident progress. I pledge my love and loyalty to* ***Jamaica land we love****. Special thanks to all my family; my sisters Joan and Annette and my brother Gary and my Mom- Ivynorah Moore from Grange Hill in the Parish of Westmoreland. Mom, I love you.*

Table of Contents

Happy Birthday My Dear................................5

Negril..6

Lion Heart..7

Go West By West End.......................................8

Lucky Dube..10

Skianne…………………………………………11

Queen of Sheba…………………………..……12

Jamaica, My Thoughts of Thee………..……....13

The Great Debate……………………….…....14

Highway 2000……………………………….…15

Aluta Continua……………………………….....16

Man on a Wear……………………………..……17

Bonfire in St. Elizabeth………………….……..18

Welcome to Jamrock……………………..…...19

The River Runs No More…………….....….....20

The Path Less Traveled…………………..…....21

Jerusalem Mountain……………………….…...22

Made in J.A.M.A.I.C.A……………………….....24

Table of Contents

Snail Mail……………………………………….25

Negril of My soul……………………………..27

Reggae, Can I Light This?............................28

Alfred's Ocean Palace…………………………29

Plant a Psalm a Day…………………………30

Dreams……………………………………….31

Nicknames…………………………………….32

Round-a-bout Negril…………………………33

I Apologize…………………………………….34

Orange Hill……………………………………35

Love in Excess………………………………36

Jamaica by Bus...38

What Makes a Country Great?……………….39

Sunset in Negril………………………………40

About the Author……………………………..42

Happy Birthday My Dear

This much I have uncovered, Jamaica was not discovered.
Yet Columbus did come around, this way. He then turned around
to see the king with much to say.
King! Let me go back, with a sack. Your riches will overlap.
The British saw the deal and begged to appeal.
Original peoples of the land scattered.

Later on they never mattered.
Africans will work till dusk, so let's make these 4,240 square miles
part of the Triangle Trade.
Nanny, Bogle and Garvey stoked the flames, then as today,
we say more fire!
Fifty years of personal gain must not go in vain.
We must work harder and be brave.
But unless we refrain from the self harm,
our long dead heroes will keep turning in their graves.

Negril

There she is my friend, my first and only love,
Speak of your troubles on a raft, roundabout a town
pristine like a dove.
Speak of lazy days, hard workers, a place to free my mind.
Talk of Rick's Café, Hedonism 11, Fisherman's Beach,
read every sign.
Cliffs on the West End, seven miles to rest in,
blue sky and Rasta love.

West End awaits the weary and the beach is quite a treat.
Talk to my friends at the Jungle, and my heart beats to a peak.
Kuyaba, Awee Mawae, De Buss, so many places to go.
White sands afoot; weeds aplenty, and dreadlocks all aglow.
If happy is as happy does and live Reggae is your show,
welcome to paradise, Irie Mon! Negril is unsurpassed in beauty
and every bit unique.

Lion Heart

Uneasy lies the head that wins the bread and messes the bed,
Uneasy lays the tie that has no home
and has to move from Negril to Naggos Head.
Unnerving is the thought that doors have locks and hinges;
that even old doors doors need keys.
The head, the feet, and the heart all need some rest
and so do these knees.
He sleeps well, albeit in uneasy slumber, with a slouch.
Uneasy lies the man with the soft voice and a mind like thunder,
I am tired and weary, if I need to rest, right now,
can I use your couch?

Go West, By West End

At high noon high temperatures flare, and taxi horns blare.
Vendors stare and blenders call out to sunbathers
in birthday suits with their rolling paper.
Those making things work toil and labor in leisure capital Jamaica.
For many, leisure is their work; and others work for leisure.
Seven miles of pride and seven days to soak up the pleasure.

At midnight all the demons come calling out to the shore.
All their stresses are floated, jerked and smoked like never before.
All their needs are packaged, sold and solicited until the sun beckons.
Where bonfires and bongs backdrop white faces
with black daughters and sons.

At sunrise, before the suits arrive to a clean beach,
where they can preach about sun and sand, and all that's noble and grand.
The bongs are bagged, the bags are gone,
and so are the white ladies and the reggae band.
Normal folks take the streets and make their rounds.

While the locks with the keys and the keys with the locks and pounds wait,

out of sight and mind, until the twilight.

When Negril arouses from a days slumber and the night comes alive. Ready?

Yah Mon, Jah know, everything alright!

Lucky Dube

High spirits guide, I glide and accept the smiles.

Long speeches and Peaches linger for a while,

the wood carving artist is called Arnie,

he lives close to the pond, what a man!

Life is like the wind, I live it and I see it. I love this Geneva land.

In time I hear the beat like a Grenade. I hear the wind,

I see the rock, but not the hand.

Smiles still my way comes, it means I am here I did not get mucky.

Dube, I made it safely through the storm,

you did too but God has called.

Jamaica, land of my birth! I did not die tonight;

time goes on for me so my new name is LUCKY.

Skianne

In But a moment of truth, I come to my senses.

In a fit or fortitude I separate my walls and my fences.

In the minute it takes to think away life's pain,

I realize if I never love another, my life will be in vain.

In but a minute I cry for a change, but what could this mean?

In but a moment you make me unhappy and I scream!

I don't need you anymore, my love is in retreat.

In but a moment, one single beat,

I shake, I awaken, and thank God it was just a dream.

Queen of Sheba

If the stars govern the earth, I know I must look up to them.

If the earth keeps turning, I want to end up in your heaven.

If heaven is real, and all your faults are yours, you are absolutely perfect.

If I have ever glimpsed a star, gazed at it from afar, you are closer yet.

Woman, as much as the earth is the Lord's, and all within.

If you are not a Queen on earth you are her next of kin.

Jamaica, My Thoughts of Thee

Like a rock Jamaicans need to be strong,
Like a rock, the land we love we must never do her wrong.
Our faults are our badges, but our heart is cockpit pure.
We believe she is the best, dare to dream, pray and always prepare.
Even if we are scared stiff, if we fail would anyone care?

Like Rockstars, we must grace the mirror and smile.
For all the cockpit countryside, St. Ann, St. Mary, Three miles.
Like a rock, we must carry our weight; ask no favors,
we have gotten many, refused a lot.
Like a rock, time is all we ask for and time is all we've got.
And sometimes I cry in my sleep and pray our strength survives.
Like a rock, the country will be stronger; we have more love to share,
but not a dime to spare.
Thanks to all who toiled for us, some gone; some still around.
We will not give up, because we stand on solid ground.

The Great Debate

Because I have messed up many times and lied.

Because I have sinned against you, no matter how hard I tried.

I have been robbed, stabbed, shot; left for dead.

Payment for my sins- aches of the feet, heart and head.

Because of you, and your sins against me,

I offer, ask and seek forgiveness so let it be.

Because of my sins, our sins; not just mine or yours,

we heal each other and come back for more.

Highway 2000

64, 65, 70 miles per hour, good! Am I going too fast? Maybe not.
Take a chance at 75, a quick glance at the clock.
I have to get into this traffic and get moving,
because I am on my way to Vere.
If you are intent on moving too slowly I beg you beware,
I need to reach my destination while my coffee is still hot.

Appleton kept me up last night; I woke up late, at 8 o'clock.
You can move fast, move over, or stop.
Here I come, or here I go at half past 8,
No thanks to any of you I am running late.

"Now on to fast track traffic,
there is an accident just north of Washington Boulevard".
Ok so much for my hurry, after all why drive hard?
You can cut in front me if you want,
We're not going anywhere fast right now, or at least I can't!

Aluta Continua

So many things to say to you Jamaica and I want to say it loud,
So many ways to pray for peace on your shores
like water from a cloud.
So many times I think I have lost the fight
as I smile and think aloud,
If I am here and you are there,
can we maintain our love across the miles?
So many times I cry in my sleep, so many times I smile,
For what does it profit a man? Fast money and mobility?
To where?
Say what you will about my land, I will say it loud and clear,
I will never leave you lonely Jamaica; I will always keep you near.

Man On a Wear

I saw him, stoic, situated and well dressed.

He saw me, and he spoke like he was taught.

We saw each other and I knew he was blessed.

He was unaware from whence he came.

He chose a place, and accepted a name.

I saw him and he looked afraid; hiding behind his lapel.

Man unaware, God bless him and remove his spell.

Bonfire in St. Elizabeth

Rock Star, star of the Elizabethan plains.
Rock hard, art of the aortas and veins.
Play hard, play like winning is about to come,
If you dare, call them out to see Sam Sara, and wait for the sun.
Rock Star, in Negril the sun is brighter,
It shines higher on the beach out west,
the land of Orange Hill and De Buss.
Rock Star of the seven mile strip you are the best, in you we trust.

Welcome to Jamrock

Good morning sunshine.

It is early in the morning, I feel the cool Mandeville breeze—

yes it's still early.

It is early in the day. And I wanted to say I love you dearly.

Before the kind dew drops vanish and the sun gets angry.

It is early in the morning, and before it goes awry,

I may need to say good morning, before the good vibes passes by,

We know not what this way comes, so I will make this moment mine.

Good morning sunshine, blessed love, thanks for your time.

The River Runs No More

The river of my childhood ran many miles through town.

In times of drought and storms and flood, it flourished all year round.

Wherever the river went from here, people claimed it as their own.

After school we played, all summer we bathed, it never let us down.

On my return from traveling far and wide,

I could not believe my eyes.

The river had left town, just like I did. It had taken to the skies.

But it never came back, not even for a visit and I could not understand why.

Did I neglect the good you did, and made you feel alone?

Did you think I left for better streams and never cared about those at home?

The river of my childhood is a lesson in disguise,

wherever in the world you roam, through journeys near and far,

those close to your heart, that add meaning to your life

must also grace your eyes.

So river of my childhood days, whether you return or not,

I promise to care for those I have in my life today, and love them quite a lot.

The Path Less Traveled

Time has come for independence, subjugated days are gone,
Time has seen us raise the dead, to help us calm the storm.
The way we handled our ancestors' lore we never kept the score.
The things they did that make us proud, our task is a quick encore.
Independent, proud and colorful now, we are a colony no more.

Time has come to smile a while, time still saves our souls.
Write a story in 1962, work hard and watch it unfold.
Time, minutes, years, date,
Understanding and love is much sweeter than hate.
Time has come to celebrate; it's 50 years to date. God bless us
with his wisdom and keep us free and safe.
As we continue proud Jamaicans all,
out of many one loving human race.

Jerusalem Mountain

I recount and remember there were 2 suitors, maybe more,
After the exchange, came the changes. August 1962,
yes they did for sure.
Taking care to build a nation strong from sea to shore.
Laughter and joy. How are you doing 50 years later my dear?
We are doing fine Montego-Bay, thanks for asking.
Not even dreary dark days and penniless thoughts could foresee.
Fear not the evil ones, love watches over me.
So what is the verdict? Diligence is good medicine,
it makes a body strong.
No matter the crisis nor the cause, we have come too far to stop.
We have worked for far too long.

Keep on climbing Jerusalem! Grow up strong Jamaica!
A mountain is a metaphor.
God bless our highest peaks, and anoint our island shore.
Jamaica 50! Who would have thought we could succeed?
We have much to be proud of and smile,
ask not what your country can do for you.

Do your diligent part. Be proud Jamaica; God speed.

Made in J.A.M.A.I.C.A

From the street corners they wandered onto fields unkempt,
A sugar cane feast from fields nearby
was the only food of which they dreamt.
Days were counted in football games, long walks,
and Bongo T's log.
The marbles kept us busy and
Barry G kept us dancing on his 2 to 6 beat.
Minutes morphed into days,
and time made the morning dew speak.

Men took their places, they grew up reluctantly,
and responsibility replaced their breadfruit feasts.
Men took their places, their faces changed, who am I?
Who is this man? Time is his yeast.
Pressure dropped for Andy, not the best Forrester, yet he saw pine.
We still smile his smile; his time is gone in flesh and blood,
but in our hearts he remains divine.
Made in Jamaica, concocted in Grange Hill,
everlasting if not in time, then where? In the mind.

Snail Mail

This bit of natural prayer in my mind,
is for friends and family that I left behind.
Who since I left to travel the world,
have died and gone to heaven before I had a chance
to see them one last, final time.

The lady that lived at the end of my street,
with the hearty hello every time we would meet.
My Uncle Bertie, A proud man with all his boastful talk,
I remember to this day his happy smile
with a brisk, purposeful walk.
The kid whose sister was my girlfriend,
who looked up to me, but ran with the wrong crowd,
and whose life came to an early end.

No final goodbyes, no words of good luck,
our relationships broken in half leaving just,
the sad news of a loved-one's untimely demise.
If only I could, one final time, look deep into their eyes,

I would accept their smiles as a present,

and their presence as an enormous prize.

Negril of my Soul

West End, Beach Road, taxi man, get a load
One stop at Awee Maway, on to De Buss, what a lively crowd!
One Mile is next with their local flair, let's stop and wait a while
Weed! Cess! Shh, whatever you want Negril will give,
no need to be so loud,

West End is the best end, but then who can compare?
Tigress, Kuyaba, Alfred's and Rick's, waste a whole day and stare,
at the world coming to a waltz in Negril. Go there and be blessed.
Law and order? Maybe. Lay low and order your cess.
Negril, at world's end, my best friend;
until we meet again—take care.

Reggae, Can I Light This?

Coconut trees swayed, the reggae band played, we all seem dazed.

Old souls and new faces drank booze and hip gazed.

The air was lazy, hazy, Cannabis wafting on the breeze.

Jerk, steamed, fried to taste, some raw; but everything to please.

One Love! Reggae lifestyle, moving to a slow Negril beat.

I stepped outside to a freezing cold!

I am in Atlanta, that club is really neat.

Alfred's Ocean Palace

Regular winds blew regular nouns,

Regular folks blew regular sounds,

One regular guy tried his regular tricks,

Regular Marley, Tosh, same white ladies, regular hits,

Regular Thursday night, Negril on show,

All new faces here, no one that I know.

Plant a Psalm a Day

When life is over and the land goes dark,
go see the maker for litigation.
But if the seed is alive, growing, it seems like hibernation.
When the farmer plants a seed, above ground there is nothing,
but below there's germination.
But if you do not play with dirt, grit and grime,
it's your palate minus salivation.
When the master is awake, sowing and planting,
in solitary refinement,
one lonely seed shall rise up from the darkness below
and bring us all salvation.

Dreams

There is a cool wind that blows around each night.

Whispering to me in my sleep, urging me to Club Twilight.

The natural mystic is flowing; there is Reggae music in my head.

As I sleep, I pray the Lord my soul to keep, hoping I am not dead.

There is an eternal calling- the voice I really dread.

Give mom a message; tell her I am at peace and final rest,

I gave it a long hard fight.

Nicknames

Some call me by my first name- Jamaica, some say Yaad,
which is my alias.
That's fine with me I do not care,
unless they are fake accents or maniacs.
I prefer to think I am a good boy, a sober 4 leaf clover,
Thinking we are still together, even though we are indeed over.
You can call me anytime my dear, my new name is brainiac.
I will hear my name because
I traded the Appleton special for an aphrodisiac.

Call my name, I will listen and respond.
If you are Jamaican, then chat Patois, I can understand,
in spite of the Reggae beat the Indika Band is playing.
Yaad man, Yardie, what a gwaan mon? What are you saying?
Please leave a message after the beep, Rick's Café here I come.
So many things to say, but not right now.

Round-about Negril

In the fourteen parishes of Jamaica, and also in Negril,
Folks talk a lot on their cell phones and boast about their thrills,
They mention London, visas, plane rides and greencards.
Miami, even New York, everywhere except their own Yard,
I have ticket stubs from all of the above, in my glove compartment,
I have seen London's west end up close
and I had the Miami apartment.
In all of this and after all the bliss I prefer Negril
and still will forever.
Negril all the time, Negril state of mind. I love Jamaica;
hook line and sinker.

I Apologize

If I have seen Wimbledon, loved Kilburn high street,
glimpsed the Ruckers in New York,
I have lived in Broward, browsed Atlanta,
borrowed Stamford's water park.
I saw the Miami Seaquarium and
shopped at the Flea Market on Sunrise Boulevard.
Taught at Georgia schools, felt the cold in December;
drank the soft water, while gas prices hit very hard.
Yet, to my regret, I have never been to Rebel Salute
or climbed Dunn's River falls.
Never to Rio Bueno, nor Lover's Leap at all.

I apologize sincerely, I have learnt within this poem,
no matter where in the world you go, there is no place like HOME.
The very next time I get a chance, I will make amends.
Embrace the land, feel the love- say hello to all my friends.
If you are like me, before time is no more, and daises call,
be sure to love those things most dear to you,
ever since you were very small.

Orange Hill

Blue rivers, green morass, cascading buds for miles,
Not Budweiser, but bud-wiser; the capital of the Cess.
The streams are clean and the hills are mean,
so do not bring empty smiles.
Purple Skunk is here, cali buds for sure, that white stuff is a mess.
Iron birds and eagles hover near, looking for a chance,
Like loving fathers to their kids, they know it is the best,
In Orange Hill, Next to Negril, you find Jamaica’s best.

Love in Excess

Four humans all of different hues, in a bitter driving cold,
each with a bit of wood around a dying fire.
Decided to play a part and risk a certain death,
they failed to see past looks and skin, at real human desire.

The first took a sideways glance; put her log back in her bag.
Her hatred hard, like a fist, covered her like a sack.
She did so quick and with frown,
because one person sitting across from her was black.

The next one rich and powerful,
thought hard but he was sure,
his log was not for this fire,
he knew the other three were poor.

The third, a poor hard-working stiff,
saw them the reason for his being dire.
So much he said aloud to them,
"the poor cannot pay for the rich man's fire"

The fourth made up his mind with just a peek,
those sinners are to blame.
His log was holy, for pure folks only,
these folks are undeserving, and their church is not the same.

An hour later their bodies stiff, the fire all but dead,
clutching logs and frowning, were found by a passing lad.
He saw the wood, he smiled but he felt gloom,
around his fire the night before, sat four homeless people, and for that
he sure was glad.

Jamaica by Bus

Start in Kingston at West Street, heading to Negril Beach Road,
Mini-bus man, we need to leave now, get a load.
We make one stop in Spanish Town to get a snack and take a break.
Soon we are passing by Old Harbor, heading for May Pen,
On to Melrose Hill, if the wind is still you see and smell the Mud Lake.
Far from Mile Gully, in the high hills of Spur Tree,
Cruising on the bypass, the lowlands of Jamaica I can see.

Anyone stopping in Santa Cruz, Luana or Black River?
No Bulla and Pear for me,
I must get Fish and Bammy when we get to the Border.
In Whitehouse, I see my family, and then back on board the ride,
my final stop is Grange Hill, but I cannot reach until,
I see Norman Manley Boulevard and West End,
and spend the night in Negril.

What Makes a Country Great?

On what makes a country great, a people brave and strong,
has been debated far and wide achieved by only some.
Of all the talks and plans galore,
for those who have done themselves proud agree on this for sure,
growth is incremental, you must work hard while others snore.

Jamaica, land of Caribbean grace, Maroon and Cockpit fame.
Independence must not become a brace;
hard work, not crime or shame.
Jamaicans home, and those away,
we pledge our love and hope,
with pride and joy, we onward toil in the upliftment of her name.

Sunset in Negril

If you have ever seen her lean against the Caribbean Sea,
thoughts oozing from her brow, a mix of sun,
sea and sand unmatched.
Visitors clamoring for a minute of her time;
in a place where no one wears a watch.
If you have ever been to Rick's Cafe,
on the lean-on-lavish west end, you may have seen him,
and he would have told you that he dreams in wide angles,
with mirrors for eyes and stones for brain waves.

He would tell you that he is always up for a few treasured
thoughts, a few hearty laughs,
and that the permanent place in his heart,
is black and gold and blue. Blue for the Caribbean Sea,
black and gold the colors of a nation of Gods and Goddesses,
and lest you forget, there is Appleton Special.
My world is round, but Negril is the very center of me.

If you have ever seen the sun, maneuvering from the east,
stroking the Blue Mountains,
caressing the Cockpit country with a whisper of a laugh
aimed at the Maroons. And by the time it gets to Negril,
it is much calmer, like water from a fountain.
Softer and more relaxed so that it can mentor the blue waters,
seven miles long, seven lions strong;
saying goodbye but for a few moments in earth time.
With a kiss that says surely I shall return in the morning.
Like Tyrone Taylor singing "From a little Cottage in Negril" I will;
always love you still.
This, my friends, is sunset in Negril.

About The Author

Mark Flemming was born in Grange Hill in the Parish of Westmoreland, Jamaica. He currently resides in the United States where he works as an educator and author. His most recent book entitled “Jamaica, my Thoughts of Thee” was done to commemorate Jamaica’s 50th year as an independent nation. His second, “Selected Poems” is also available. He writes extensively about Jamaica, and his life growing up close to the world famous Negril 7 mile beach strip. He also writes about the American lifestyle and history juxtaposed against the writings of those who had similar views about peace in the world we inhabit and woven around his own ideas about peace, love and justice for all mankind. Please send feedback to mr_mflemming@yahoo.com or tweet @negril_mayor.

www.ingramcontent.com/pod-product-compliance
Ingram Content Group UK Ltd.
Pitfield, Milton Keynes, MK11 3LW, UK
UKHW041905190726
13854UKWH00003B/1099